PF

Infinite Possibility

"Katherine Jegede's great book is challenging and thought provoking. There's no holding back or compromising in Katherine's vision of Neville and her bold action plan to make your life really work."

—Jim Lefter, CEO, The New Thought Channel

"In *Infinite Possibility*, Katherine Jegede faithfully and dynamically reintroduces the ideas and techniques of Neville Goddard to a new generation. Whether you are, like me, a longtime lover of Neville's work or a newcomer, this book provides you with an entirely fresh estimate of how much power these ideas can bring into your life. It is an invaluable addition to the growing rediscovery of Neville's work." —Mitch Horowitz, PEN Award–winning author of *Occult America* and *The Miracle Club*

"Finding meaning and transformation in life's inevitable suffering is too often ignored in New Thought, but no longer thanks to the courageous Katherine Jegede. 'You create your reality' can be a too easily applied Band-Aid for life's horrors unless you've lived it. Katherine doesn't take the easy road. She faced horror in her own life, asked the hard questions, and came out on the other side by arguing with, testing, and applying the teachings of her beloved Neville. This book, *Infinite Possibility*, is her gift to us, but only if we follow her lead by arguing with and testing the teachings to make them our own."

—Harv Bishop, HarvBishop.com,

editor of *Can New Thought Be Saved?*

"Katherine Jegede is a forceful proponent for the teachings of the great metaphysician Neville Goddard."

—Paul Selig, author of *The Book of Mastery*

and *I Am the Word*

INFINITE
POSSIBILITY

How to Use the Ideas of Neville Goddard
to Create the Life You Want

KATHERINE JEGEDE

A TARCHERPERIGEE BOOK

An imprint of Penguin Random House LLC
375 Hudson Street
New York, New York 10014

Most TarcherPerigee books are available at special quantity discounts
for bulk purchase for sales promotions, premiums, fund-raising, and
educational needs. Special books or book excerpts also can be created
to fit specific needs. For details, write: SpecialMarkets@
penguinrandomhouse.com.

ISBN 9780143132479

Printed in the United States of America
1 3 5 7 9 10 8 6 4 2

Book design by Katy Riegel

*This book is dedicated to my darling husband, Deji,
who embodies the beauty of life and
who reminds me daily of who it is I have always been.*

*I give my deepest, most special thanks to my mother,
who from the earliest moments of my life set a shining example.
Mum, you inspire me always, I love you.*

*I must also thank my dad, my hero and my friend.
And to my siblings I say thank you for your
incredible support of a writing career
that was believed in before it was seen.*

*I also wish to thank Mitch Horowitz,
whose own work, support, and outstanding ideas have meant
more to me than he'll possibly ever know. And kind thanks
to Heather Brennan, for patience and email-answering
above and beyond the call of duty.*

So I bring you a message to make you conscious: man must awake from the dream where he is simply an automaton. He moves like a machine, then he begins to awake and when he awakes then he is not that man at all that he seemingly in the past played for eternity. He awakes into a new being, a new man.

–Neville Goddard

CONTENTS

Contents

Your Great Experiment

by Mitch Horowitz

As someone who has written extensively on the history of New Thought and other mystical movements, I dread one (and only one) interview question: "What voices in contemporary New Thought excite you?" The honest answer is: almost none.

New Thought and positive-mind philosophy today have lost their bravery. Almost all of their books make tepid or vague claims, and almost all of their exponents vacillate between sloganeering and bland generalizing.

Almost.

An exception is Kate Jegede. She writes with the passion of the pioneers, especially Neville Goddard, whose methods receive a practical and dynamic re-exploration in this book.

As a student of Neville's thought, Kate—like any true spiritual experimenter—has nowhere to hide. A practical spiritual philosophy either works or it doesn't. That was Neville's challenge to modern life—and it is a challenge that Kate confronts here with courage, clarity, and practicality. Her book is about trying things; and measuring results.

As you will see from her introduction, Kate has worked intimately with Neville's methods, and has repeatedly tested his audacious and inspiring principle that God is the human imagination. Through times of deep personal sorrow and extraordinary triumph, Kate reached the informed, radical conclusion: Neville was right. You will find that she uses no dodges or slogans, and has weathered immense personal challenges to reach this conclusion.

Kate divides Neville's methods into simple, powerful chapters, each of which lays out a specific technique and guides you in exactly how to use it. She, like Neville, asks no one to take anything on faith or goodwill. Rather, Kate brings her own insights and personal experiences to weigh on Neville's ideas, and offers irresistibly simple but dramatic methods to test the ultimate power of your mind. Try these ideas or forget them. The choice is yours.

I feel confident that if you've read this far in this foreword you will accept Neville's and Kate's challenge, and will work with the methods in this book. Most of us have lost the ability of personal ethical and spiritual experimentation. We nest within a world of social and news media, most of which affirms whatever we already believe, and mitigates against our asking: What if there's another way?

How do you or I know that a moral or mystical idea is to be taken seriously, or that our lives are bound by certain parameters, unless we challenge our conduct through new systems of thought? It is not enough to find a given idea appealing; its efficacy will remain unknown unless we attempt to live by it. And that is what this book is for.

Nothing in Kate's book will rupture or divide you from your personal obligations and relationships. This book contains strictly inner experiments, though each is geared toward outward results (which is the only authentic way to measure an inner experiment).

Ralph Waldo Emerson wrote in his journals on January 15, 1857: "This good which invites me now is visible & specific. I will at least embrace it this time by way of experiment, & if it is wrong certainly God can in some manner signify his will in future. Moreover I will guard against evil consequences resulting to others by the vigilance with which I conceal it." Put differently, experiments of the mind allow for correction, and do not endanger the well-being of others, or the good that already is. That is the spirit in which we proceed here.

In approaching these ideas, remember: you are not required to join anything or quit anything; change the outer labels of your life; rearrange personal relations; or pay money or tributes to anyone. In using these techniques, you are working solely within the exquisitely private world of your mind. And in so doing, you may discover that your mind is all the world.

A PEN Award–winning historian and publisher, **Mitch Horowitz** is the author of books including *Occult America, One Simple Idea,* and *Mind as Builder.*

PREFACE

I HOPE THIS BOOK aids you in understanding the core principles of Metaphysics and sets the process of self-renewal in motion. I aim to inspire you to put all of its theories to the test, and, in so doing, to carve out for yourself a path to magnificence in life that culminates in a completely radical psychological transformation that is tangibly evidenced.

If you put these theories to the test, you will discover the truth of Metaphysical Law for yourself and there will be absolutely no limit to what you can achieve both in your own life and in the lives of others.

If you believe you need to change the world, give that up at once; you need only to change your relationship to the things in the world. In doing this you will discover the secret of causation and the true meaning of life.

The exercises are not difficult to do; they are written so as to make them accessible to everyone. The principles upon which they are based, however, are alive, ageless, and intelligent and hide themselves from anyone unwilling to move from their present premise of belief to the realm of unlimited possibilities.

One benefit of testing Metaphysical Law is the discovery of an ability to understand and interpret biblical text. Because the Bible is spiritually discerned, to understand it you will need to have developed communication between your inner and outer cognitive faculties. The Bible is a psychological document having no basis in religious dogma and is one of the greatest phenomena known to mankind. Understanding it will transform your life.

Best of all, you will also discover the greater you, the being as yet unseen by objective sight but which is responsible for every physical effect and the outward physical projection of every imagined act.

This book is not lengthy, and deliberately so. It makes no effort to persuade the reader as to the truth of Metaphysical Law by labored arguments. It simply sets out the core teachings of Metaphysics, sticking to the salient points. It builds, line upon line, precept upon precept, here a little, there a little, and is in whole a complete document of practical guidance for the achievement of any ambition, with guaranteed results.

INTRODUCTION

I STAND BY THE ideas in this book—because they have worked for me. But I didn't merely have faith in them, I proved them by result.

In fact, at one time I wanted nothing to do with the teachings of Neville Goddard, but in my effort to prove him wrong I began to experiment with his theories, and they changed my life.

I fondly remember a positive and vibrant early childhood in the northwest London suburb I was born in. My five siblings were my friends, and my parents my bedrock, my mother in particular.

I idolized my mother. I watched her closely during my early years. A highly respected educator and teacher trainer, she ran a number of after-school and weekend activities for needy children, yet never neglected her own at home.

By contrast, my father, who was in my view a little unpredictable and somewhat dictatorial, played a much quieter role. To be fair, he did spend most of this period of my life working abroad. But, while I did enjoy his brief visits, when he returned home on a permanent basis I found the shift in dynamic difficult to adjust to.

I believe that my relationship with my father played a significant role in my spiritual search. He was (and still is) a Freemason and a deeply religious man, who was brought up in the Jewish faith. I remember being fascinated by the menorah, the Hebrew language, the robes, the rituals, the bags for the tallit, the tefillin, and the books covered in gold lettering. I wasn't permitted to touch these things, but I would question him constantly about them. My appetite for mysticism was not only actively encouraged by my father, but in part also fed by him.

There wasn't a vast amount of money available during my childhood but there was orchestra or hockey practice, pets, arts and crafts, outings, and riding my bike with the other kids in the neighborhood.

I would often ask my mother how she managed to look after us and give us so many wonderful treats, and she would always tell me that all it took was an active imagination. Later in life I came to understand exactly what she meant, even if she didn't fully appreciate the significance of her words at the time.

Imagining has always played a role in my life, at times inadvertently so. Somehow as a child my instinct was: if you wanted something you had to focus on it already being yours.

When I was six I wanted a hamster. It was all I could think about, and I remember that I played with my imaginary hamster every day.

My hamster's name was Chewbacca, or Chewy for short. I knew what he looked like, I knew exactly how he smelled, how soft his fur was, how his tiny claws scratched when he ran along my arms, how much he ate, and on and on. My brother Nicholas loved to tease me about my imaginary hamster, but I was resolute, and even at my young age I couldn't explain how real he was, I only knew that nothing would convince me that he was not. In the end I had to make a hamster out of a dustcloth just to stop the teasing, but the dustcloth hamster could never compare to my magnificent pet, even if he only lived inside my head.

I had sequestered a shallow white plastic laundry basket to be the hamster's cage, so strong was my conviction. I even asked my mother to buy herself a new basket. She said no, and so we shared hers in the end.

And then one Saturday morning after breakfast my

mother told me to get dressed, she was taking me out for a treat. You may have already guessed that the treat was a visit to the local pet shop. Needless to say, I could have fainted.

I don't think I'll ever forget that day; I am so happy that my memories of it are still so vivid.

Back then I didn't know what any of it meant. I certainly didn't make the connection between my imaginal activity and the pet I came to cherish for the next seven years. But it's memories like these, simple happy childhood reminiscences, that I can recall now as illustrative of the theories I live by today.

My childhood home was a place of love, fun, and friendship, but in spite of this, daily life in our respectable, almost exclusively English neighborhood tended to be a little isolating.

I believe it was this experience that led to my mother's joining the church I would go on to spend the rest of my childhood in. The congregation provided the welcoming sense of community we lacked on our own doorstep.

I didn't enjoy going to church. I found Sunday school inane and the routine of the services odd. There was some relief when my mom took over the teaching, but her radical attempt to introduce New Thought authors and their ideas to the children made her position untenable, and she was asked to stand down.

By the time I reached my teens, I had decided absolutely that church was not for me. I found it horribly restrictive. Endless rules and double standards.

I was an expressive, creative young person who couldn't abide being told how to dress, or that dating was strictly forbidden, that celebrating birthdays was paganist, that I was not allowed to watch certain types of programs on television or listen to certain types of music. And being told what to eat, or who I could and could not be friends with, made my blood boil.

I questioned my mother relentlessly, determined to know why we were members of the church when she herself had no interest in the doctrine being taught. She had for as long as I could remember embraced an alternative path as a truth seeker.

The ideas she shared with us (with me in particular), those of Neville Goddard, James Allen, Erich von Däniken, Norman Vincent Peale, Florence Scovel Shinn, and other progenitors of positive thinking and New Thought, were wildly at odds with the traditional approach to religion we were practicing.

I don't remember Mom ever giving me an answer that completely satisfied me—beyond something vague about our needing the church's society, protection, and friendship—and by age fifteen I stopped, for the first time, going altogether. I would later grudgingly attend church when the effort of trying to argue my way out of it became too much, but I hated it. I hated everything about it. I found some relief in the music department, playing the keyboard and later the organ. I loved organ music and I was able to lose myself in the activity until I at last got my driver's license and could finally do as I pleased.

I often heard my parents discuss my church attendance. My mother was on my side absolutely, arguing my right to choose, while my father, who had himself made significant sacrifices in converting to Christianity (he would later revert back to his original faith), felt that attendance was nonnegotiable. In the end they both agreed to let me decide.

I knew that I wasn't liked by senior members of the church, I had been told so by many of them in no uncertain terms, but I didn't care. In the end I had to do what was right for me, and religion was definitely not right for me.

Being the only non-churchgoing member of my family was a lonely business at first. My mother and I were still extremely close, but my stand regarding church had inexplicably put a dampener on our wonderful New Thought conversations.

She was still reading and seeking, as far as I knew, but doing so without me. Feeling slightly betrayed, I decided to give up on anything even remotely related to the supernatural or spiritual. I had turned my back on organized religion and nothing would persuade me to take it up again.

When at nineteen I got to university, I met a group of humanists whose atheist position really intrigued me. I was open to a new way of life—a guilt-free, godless existence backed up by science. It was great to think that for the first time in my life I could legitimately believe whatever I wanted, although there was something about the humanist argument that I found sterile.

Giving up my faith in pursuit of a more fulfilling and satisfying life was proving ironically miscalculated. I graduated from university with disappointing results, but having already worked as a staff writer for the world's leading science journal *Nature*, I knew I could write. I also knew what I wanted to do: I would build a career in broadcasting, specializing in public engagement with science.

Following my graduate year of academic research at Oxford, I did an internship with the BBC Science Unit, then left the UK at age twenty-three to live and work in Switzerland as a science communicator for the World Health Organization. By all appearances I was living the dream, but I was deeply unhappy.

I returned to the UK, and at age twenty-five took a string of temp jobs, first with the Royal Academy of Arts, then with the UK Parliament, then at Christie's Auction House, then with the Queen's Honors List Committee, and finally as a property manager for the Saudi royal family. It was heady stuff. I was surrounded by immense wealth and some incredibly influential people, but nothing about the experiences or the offers that came my way could inspire or motivate me.

I was taking the time to seriously contemplate my career—I wanted to write—and it was at this time that my mother reintroduced me to the teachings of Neville Goddard.* She told me to go back to the copy of *The Five Lessons* she'd first given me more than a decade earlier— and this time I read it.

I fell in love with Neville, instantly, indescribably. Something inside of me stirred.

I started collecting Neville's books, devouring everything he'd ever written. I trusted him even when his words made no earthly sense to me, and I always retained an open mind.

Then, just over a year later, at age twenty-six, disaster struck. I was the victim of a horrible crime.

I remember the day it happened as though it were yesterday. I got home afterward and sat on the steps in front

---

* Many of Neville's lectures are available online, and in some cases I refer to the name of a lecture as it is popularly known online; it is generally searchable by that title.

of the house, stunned. My head was spinning. By the time I went inside I couldn't speak. I went to my bedroom, barely breathing.

I didn't cry, but I reached into my handbag next to me on the bed and pulled out my Bible and the copy of *The Power of Awareness* by Neville that I had been carrying around with me.

I remember putting the Bible on the pillow and staring at Neville's book in my shaking hands.

I was very quiet all evening; I didn't eat, and at some point I fell asleep. It was very late when I woke up and first attempted to telephone the police, about two a.m. I was so thirsty, and still shaking with fear. But fear quickly turned to anger, an immense anger that suddenly and viciously sprang up inside me. I was angry with Neville.

It may seem inconceivable that I could have felt that way, but you have to understand that during that last year I had been living almost exclusively by Neville's teachings. I had in fact begun to build my life on them. Neville's philosophy had become my religion and I felt very superior about that. The fact that I was now a crime victim made me sick with anxiety. I felt incredibly lost, and in addition to that I was engulfed by shame.

As a devout follower of Neville's I had come to believe that my thoughts and my thoughts alone created my life, and yet as a twenty-six-year-old crime victim, accepting that my thoughts had actualized this particular event was too much to ask. Neville had to go.

I had to distance myself from Neville. I couldn't run the risk of anyone throwing his philosophy in my face. I couldn't bear the thought of being called a fool for giving up church, for giving up religion.

Looking back at that time in my life, it is the surrealistic nature of the experience that stands out for me most. Sitting in a police station alone, terrified as I made my statement, I felt as if I weren't really there. It was all so official and draining.

The warnings about making a false statement, the threat of prosecution if I was found to be lying, my protests about wanting to keep things private, my fears for my reputation, the impact on my family when they found out the truth—it was all too much to take. I wanted to disappear.

I remember arriving home after my third police interview, dry-mouthed and headachy, feeling hopeless and in despair. My thoughts, which had already grown dark, were exceptionally depressive that day. Somewhere in the depths of my mind I knew I had to recover.

That same evening I decided to read Neville's 1969 lecture *The First Principle*, which deals with concepts of innate spirituality. I can't recall why I chose to do this. It seemed wildly at odds with my determination to be rid of

Neville. While discussing the lecture with my mother (who had been quietly and privately assisting me), I became very snippy and aggressive. I was trying to pick holes in Neville's theory, and was searching for some inconsistency, some error that would prove that he was a fraud. I also hoped—and failed—to convince my mother of this too.

I told myself that once I did this, I would be able to get on with life in the real world.

The following day and for the rest of that week I read *The First Principle* countless times. I don't recall that I absorbed any of it, but I do vividly remember doing my best to ignore the comfort and sense of security the words seemed to be giving me.

I fixated on one particular line and lay in bed awake at night constantly repeating it to myself. It was, "Are you really God, is it really true?"

This wasn't an attempt to reboot my interest in Neville's work; at best I suppose I was trying to retest his theory in an effort to disprove it. I would say that it was at this point that I began to earnestly experiment with Neville's theories.

I don't remember how long I did this, and I can't say that the heavens opened or that the earth shook under my feet. What I can say is that before I knew it I had begun to experience the teachings of Neville in a deeper way.

His story about the discovery of the human imagination as God was becoming my experience. I felt it to be true deep down.

And that is all that happened.

Without realizing it, I had undergone a spiritual transformation born out of my pain and hopelessness, and I had received irrefutable spiritual validation of my inner change.

I moved on to studying Neville's 1969 lecture *The Secret of Causation* in which he details the ways in which imagination creates reality and provides an explanation for why we seem to be the victims of our manifested ideas. Ultimately I wanted to know exactly how and why I had gone through such hell. Although this lecture didn't provide all the answers I was seeking, I concluded that the circumstances leading to my misfortune had a traceable origin—a preoccupation with a particular fear that had indiscriminately drawn into my world the very undesirable circumstances I had envisioned.

According to Neville, there is only one power in the universe out of which all things emanate. Not a necessarily good source and a separate evil one, but one universal source bending in obedience to the creative will of men and women everywhere. The how remains a mystery, but this eternal fact is nonetheless true. As soon as I was able to feel and *accept* this to be true, I was free. I also developed a personal method for forgiving the person who had wronged me.

I wish I knew every detail of the entire process and could relay them here, but I simply cannot. I was determined to regain control of my life and recover from the torment I was suffering, and this determination underpinned every action I took.

A few short months after the aforementioned event, I was the victim of a vicious campaign of slander initiated by members of my former church and was going through other serious challenges. The more awful the external struggle got, the more determined and focused I became. All of the events together culminated in a divine confluence of teaching me about my inner strength.

This explanation may not entirely satisfy you, and that is quite all right. I only ask that you be open-minded and willing enough to put the theories that I lay out in the following chapters to the test. I am confident that everything I say can be proven by the testing.

During my recovery I found great strength in Neville's teaching on revision, specifically our innate ability to literally undo the effects of past experiences by mentally traveling back in time and altering them. In his 1954 lecture *The Pruning Shears of Revision*, Neville provides a compelling argument in support of this challenging concept. I explain exactly how to use this particular principle later in the book, but armed with this new knowledge I was able to let go of the fear I had felt for most of my life.

When I went through the court process because of the crime I mentioned earlier, I did so with an internal strength that I could neither explain nor attribute to any source other than my human imagination—God himself. Crucially, I envisioned a successful outcome, which was the most difficult thing that I had ever had to do. That things went well for me meant that, at least for the time being, I was absolutely certain about the truth of Neville's words.

In 2010, I met my husband, and reading Neville became a dedicated daily practice. I wasn't seeking any particular guidance, but I was acutely aware that I felt alive and positive whenever I read his books, and down and vulnerable when I did not.

Since that day I have practiced Neville's techniques* religiously, although I have modified them in little ways that best suit my temperament. The result has been a personalized system for the conscious creative use of my imagination that has never failed me.

It is absolutely true—because I have proven it to be so— that I can go into any environment and, no matter how

---

* The exercises in each chapter are based on a range of techniques as taught by Neville during his lectures and in his books. The reader is taken through the process step by step in a way that allows for personalization of the techniques without diminishing their effectiveness.

daunting things may appear, everything and everyone around me is subject to the use of my imagination.

When I decided that I wanted to host my own television show I turned to Neville's teaching, immersing myself mentally into a career I knew nothing about and had no experience in. I needed to use what I knew to get the outcome that I wanted.

I am very shy by nature, and I would never have been able to audition on camera in front of television executives, a thing I had never done before, without first imagining that I was fantastic and exactly what they were looking for.

I was up against a large group of people who wanted the job just as much as I did, some of whom were hosts who had a great deal of experience, but I sustained the feeling that the job was mine.

In the end I hosted two series of an award-winning science show that was hugely successful and led to some incredible offers. I met many wonderful people and enjoyed a wide range of life-changing experiences, which I attribute entirely to a practical application of Neville's teachings.

I decided to place my burgeoning TV career on hold because I wanted to travel and ultimately write.

I am proud of my conviction concerning the truth of this book, and I am perfectly willing to face ridicule. I feel absolutely no embarrassment about the fact that I have discovered the reality of God for myself, and I am willing to share this message with everyone.

I now have the resources to revive my television career whenever I want, if that is what I want, because I have proven to myself that imagination creates reality, and I will never be without Neville again.

Today, as I look back over my time studying Neville's teachings, I am aware of moments of immense joy but also moments of deep sorrow, and one might ask where that leaves me in terms of my search.

My answer is this. The teachings of Neville are an indelible, practical part of my life. Through them I have found my imagination to be God. (And if the word *God* offends you, use another; I use it because of its meaning to me.) My search for truth doesn't lie within a particular theology, but it is a journey of self-exploration that is expansive, organic, and dynamic. I am constantly aware of an infinite source from which to learn. I don't know what I don't know and I am always open to know more.

The sorrow and joy are by-products of events that have happened along the way, contributing to the enrichment of my life. What Neville has done is to make real self-discovery possible.

My life's experience has inspired me to choose Metaphysics as taught by Neville over all else. I have been taught not only to live graciously and nobly, but also how to do so. I have proven to myself beyond all doubt how a change in mood results in a change in circumstances, and because I have done so by testing, nothing can shake my knowingness. It is this that urges me to share these particular methods with others in my own unique way.

The breadth of our daily experiences may be thought of as incidental to any teaching on faith or a system of belief, but in my experience the two are not mutually exclusive. Confusion arises because we place attention on others' experiences rather than our own. The world is a schoolroom that we have been placed in for one purpose only, and that is to change ourselves. We are here to experience the evolution of the soul, and this is an entirely individual event. If this explanation doesn't satisfy you, then set it aside for now. The beauty of Metaphysics lies in its transformative power, which shows its effects when we least expect them.

Neville teaches that as we change, the world around us (being purely imagined) changes to reflect our psychological state. In his 1948 lecture series titled *Five Lessons*, Neville goes into great detail about the importance of addressing our own consciousness when we want to change the circumstances of our lives overall. These lectures are perhaps his most instructively practical. The world becomes paradisiacal as we achieve paradise inwardly, but it is just as capable of being a place of torment when we fail to use our imagination constructively.

Does this mean that mental causation is solely responsible for our experience, and, if so, what about the other forces of nature at play? Well, if we are capable of believing in the sovereignty of imagination (God himself) and that creation in its entirety exists in the mind, then we can quite possibly also accept that the world around us is our mental activity projected onto the screen of space. On that basis, sole mental causation becomes easier to grasp.

But if not, then put first things first. Continue to hold others around you accountable for what they do to you and believe in a physical world of unalterable fact, acting under a plethora of universal invisible laws; this is true and there is nothing at all wrong with that. Just be willing to allow experience to teach you what the truth actually is, that all things are subject to imagination. Faith follows results.

And that is the true purpose of this book. Its aim is to give the reader an insight into the eternity that lives inside us all, not just to make mention of this unlimited power but to make the power available and thus valuable for the rest of your life.

INFINITE
POSSIBILITY

CHAPTER 1

=

Metaphysics

METAPHYSICS IS ALL of the underlying theoretical principles of creation. It is not merely concerned with the world you inhabit, but with everything that exists: that which is seen and known to you and that which is unseen and not known to you. It underpins every atom, it is absolute causation, and its true purpose is to bring about the rebirth of the soul of man—in other words, a radical psychological change in every individual.

This change, demonstrated by a sequence of spiritual and physical events, builds and builds, culminating in an exceptional empyreal event.

Unlike religious dogma open to interpretation, the principles of Metaphysics are singular, constant, and unmodifiable. They don't require any special knowledge or character trait, they are totally dependable, they are for your absolute good, but they are also only truly known through experience.

Anyone who wishes to know Metaphysics' theories and benefit from them must first be willing to put the principles of Metaphysics most rigorously to the test. Without personal experience, practical application, and physical evidence, these principles have no value.

Let us begin, then, with a summary of the three main ideas of Metaphysics. These ideas are ancient but they are highly practical in nature and serve as a guide for garnering a trenchant understanding of this enormous subject.

1. SELF-OBSERVATION. Before we can undergo a psychological change, we must become aware of the one to be changed, and we do this by keenly and uncritically observing our reactions to life. Many people are as yet unaware that there exists an inextricable link between our reactions and the conditions of our lives. This is because our reactions form the body of one's true self, which is our state of consciousness. It is our state of consciousness that is responsible for the circumstances of our lives, and once we are aware of our reactions, we are in a position to change them.

It is vital to note that only through self-observation can one of the most crucial discoveries of self be made—specifically, that we are the cause of that which displeases us. We are all quite accustomed to blaming others, blaming the circumstances and conditions of life for our unhappiness, and we are shocked when we discover that it was nothing more than—in Metaphysical-speak—our own deceitfulness that made us "suspicious of others."*

This trait of deceitfulness is a condition of our nature that tends to look outward for explanations and must be accepted before any transformation can occur.

> Man surrounds himself with the true image of
> himself . . . what we are, that only can we see.
>
> —*Emerson*

Exercise

Relax in whichever way you choose, as long as you are still and in a comfortable position. Close your eyes, and breathe deeply and evenly. Once you feel calm and undisturbed, simply begin to notice your

---

* Neville Goddard—INTA Bulletin "New Thought," 1953.

thoughts. What are the predominant ideas in your mind? How do you feel about what you are thinking? Notice what you think about on a daily basis and your feelings and reactions. These are the feelings that you most easily and often identify with. You may want to write down some of your thoughts. Repeat this exercise as often as necessary until you feel you are aware of your present state of consciousness.

2. CLARITY OF THOUGHT (DEFINITION OF AIM). Knowing exactly what it is you want—to be, do, or possess—is the crucial next step on the path to the attainment of your aims. Always think in terms of clarity of form. The clearer the image, the easier it becomes to physicalize, because your feelings toward it become stronger. Intensity of feeling is a magic ingredient. The stronger the feeling, the greater the internal commitment to make it your preeminent thought.

Even if you are entirely new to this ideology, I urge you not to put a limit on your aim. Creation is finished; you could not imagine something if it did not already exist. Rather than creating for ourselves out of "thin air," we come into contact with different aspects of creation that we go on to express. If you doubt me, then try to think of something that does *not* already exist in consciousness.

Logic and reason are the enemies of success in the world of the Metaphysical, so don't concern yourself with how your aim will become a reality; simply put the theory to the test. It will not fail you.

Exercise

Now knowing—having observed yourself—who you are, you must formulate a clear aim. Know exactly who it is you desire to be. While in a relaxed frame of mind, define the person that would exist in place of who you presently are. Then spend the day observing your reactions relative to this aim. By maintaining a clear aim, you are creating for yourself a potential new state of consciousness having its own reactions.

If your aim is to be respected, valued, wealthy, generous, or in excellent health, your reactions to the day's events will tell you whether you are walking in this state of consciousness or not. For example, a person conscious of good health isn't anxious or concerned about being ill. A person conscious of wealth does not get anxious over bills. "Assume" you are the person you desire to be by imagining what your reactions would be were your desire already a fact.

Your commitment to your aim will in time confirm your state of consciousness to you with an adjustment of the circumstances and conditions of your life. Your external environment always reflects the internal.

3. DETACHMENT. Detachment is both a willingness and an ability to separate oneself from the present state of consciousness in order to appropriate another. Having clearly defined your aim, you must detach from your present state of consciousness in order to take on the new consciousness contained within your aim.

This may seem strange at first, and you may feel powerless to stem the tide of negative thinking. This is because our reactions, our moods, our thoughts have felt like the most natural, spontaneous thing in the world. In reality we have simply become accustomed to them through habit. Have you ever considered why life seems so cyclical, why you seem unable to rid yourself of familiar problems and issues despite your best efforts? You have become identified with a particular state of consciousness wherein these things have their natural life. We must therefore practice detachment daily in order to break free.

Exercise

If you find yourself reacting to things that are not in accordance with your aim, stop it at once. Occupy your mind with other thoughts. Let nothing disturb the perfect image you have placed there.

Remain vigilant, observe your reactions constantly, and eliminate unwanted reactions by taking your attention away from any thought or feeling that does not conform to your ideal.

Metaphysics, its true purpose, and the road to mastery are rooted in these core ideas: self-observation, clarity of thought, and detachment.

Know who you are, then ask yourself what it is you want. Lastly, practice daily the art of detachment, which, once habitual in you, can be used repeatedly to bring about an inner separation between yourself and any undesirable state. Repeat this process, and sooner or later you will move into a deeper and more expansive reading of the Law of Consciousness. It is far more useful if you develop your own inner awareness through experience rather than through study. Remember, as within, so without.

We cannot expect life to be different as long as we persist in reacting to the same things. The practice of separating yourself from negative ideas, thoughts, and emotions in the midst of the turbulence of life will in short order produce a new set of conditions and circumstances.

Get ready to rise!

CHAPTER 2

Magic Mirror

WHEN YOU LOOK in the mirror, if you are dissatisfied with the image reflected back, don't accept it, change it. If you look in the mirror and, unhappy with what you see reflected there you walk away and do nothing, you are sure to be confronted with the same thing later.

The same applies to the psychological state. In the practice of Metaphysics, however, we are not restricted to external adjustments, which are temporary and incapable of bringing about lasting change; rather, we are invited to change the internal image and watch as the world around us molds itself in accordance with our desires.

Whether you realize it or not, the face you see in the mirror is the mask of God. You may find this hard to believe, since you can only see the mortal and not the immortal. But the being unseen by human eyes is the one doing the work. Have confidence in the fact that there is much more to you than you know, and as such the true scope of your capabilities is far in excess of what you presently believe it to be.

If the word *God* offends you, use another, perhaps *mind, subconscious,* or *love.* Name your immortal aspect whatever you wish; the most important thing at this point is proving this theory through testing. I use the word *God* because I understand its meaning.

Exercise

Imagine you are looking into a mirror and seeing yourself; notice how you feel. If you find it difficult to see clear mental images, do not worry, simply relax and *imagine* that you are seeing clearly. There is no point in getting frustrated if what you are trying to do seems difficult at first. Most skills take time to develop, but they do develop with practice.

After spending a few moments looking at yourself, close your mental eyes and open them again, this time seeing the one you wish to see reflected there. Notice how you feel. Relax by breathing deeply and evenly. You are attempting to hold the image without effort, which requires letting go of resistance. If your mind wanders, bring it back. Spend only a few minutes doing this exercise, trying your best not to make it an effort of will. When you repeat the exercise, do not imagine your present self right away, but go straight to the image of your destined being. In time, you will become used to seeing your ideal, which will replace the person you are presently aware of being.

Make a habit of looking into the mirror of the mind and seeing the one you wish to see reflected back. The image may not feel natural at first, and you may be inclined to dismiss it, but if you are double-minded you will not succeed. To be double-minded means to act as one who, seeing his face in a physical mirror, walks away and instantly forgets what he looks like. Grow steadfast by bringing the image to mind over and over again until it takes on the sense of reality.

CHAPTER 3

———
——

Inverse Transformations

THE ART OF prayer is a key component of the practice of Metaphysics, and, as with the other skills to be acquired, it needs practice.

Prayer has nothing to do with uttering words into the air or murmuring to some divine being separated from you. All of the pageantry, ritual, and ceremony associated with prayer have been invented to give it an air of importance, but there is no physical requirement pertinent to success.

Prayer can mean different things to different people. To many it is the making of petitions to God or some other object of worship, asking for what they want or what they feel they need. To others it is an act of spiritual communion with God or an object of worship for the purpose of devotion, thanksgiving, or supplication. I am sure that there are yet further definitions of prayer. If you are already accustomed to some form of prayer you may have practiced this most valuable exercise completely ignorant of the laws that govern it—and, having achieved the psychological attitude necessary for results, you might have misattributed the outcomes to your actions.

In essence, prayer is faith permeated with understanding, and is thus imbued with that quality of motion that faith alone does not ordinarily possess.

Understanding prayer, then, we move on to the Law of Inverse Transformations (or the Law of Reversibility), which is the bedrock upon which the claims made pertaining to prayer stand.

The Law of Inverse Transformations is universal and is repeated constantly throughout Metaphysical teaching. It states that all transformations of force are reversible. In simplest terms—and, for example, the relationships between heat and motion, motion and sound, electricity and magnetism are reversible—one can produce the other.

This law is of utmost importance, in that it enables an inverse transformation of a verified direct transformation.

For evidence of this, one need only look into the discoveries of speech-recording apparatus or friction as a source of electricity.

How, then, does the Law of Inverse Transformations help the Metaphysical student?

An answered prayer produces an unmistakable feeling (a psychological state of consciousness) of the desire fulfilled. In other words, the feeling you have once something you desired has become real and is now in your possession.

On that basis, the Law of Inverse Transformations allows that, by evoking within the self the feeling that would be yours were your desire realized, that which you desire must become real.

Biblical text stipulates that we pray believing we have already received, which is in fact the esoteric interpretation of the text.

If possession produces a specific feeling, the feeling must produce the possession as long as the feeling is evoked and sustained.

Exercise

In a happy, relaxed state of mind, ask yourself, "How would I feel if _____ were now real?" Wait and notice what you feel in response. The sensation may be subtle at first, but if you keep your attention on it, it will intensify. Hold the feeling with your attention until it feels quite natural to you.

You may also bring to mind that which you wish to express, and experience its possession in imagination. I will revisit later the proper technique for doing this (Chapter 9, "The Human Body and Metaphysics"), but for now I invite you to hear, feel, and see the most likely natural outcomes associated with the successful realization of your desire. If a new job is your goal, sit at the desk, or perform some activity that confirms you are now in the role. Hear the voices of your colleagues or the voice of some loved one congratulating you on your success. Persist in this state until it takes on the definite notes of reality.

The Law of Inverse Transformations requires only that you evoke and sustain the feeling of your realized desire until your desire is realized.

CHAPTER 4

Motor Element Thoughts

*An idea which is only an idea does nothing and produces nothing;
it only acts if it is felt, if it is accompanied by an effective state, if it
awakens tendencies, that is to say motor elements.*

—Théodule-Armand Ribot,
The Psychology of the Emotions

NOT ALL THOUGHTS are productive. The thoughts
that do and produce nothing are, as Ribot explains,
unaccompanied by an effective state and thereby do not
trigger motor elements—the motor neurons of the dia-
phragm and the intercostal muscles of respiration.

In lay-speak, if the stimulus triggers no "gut reaction,"
sometimes referred to as stimulation of the solar plexus,
it is unlikely to give rise to a physical correlate.

If you overhear some idle gossip or read a newspaper
article that worries you and you react with an involuntary
movement of the aforementioned region of your abdomen,

your reaction will fulfill itself in what you are confronted by tomorrow.

Remember, you are God, as his creation, clothed in human form. A response that is powerful enough makes an impression on consciousness (Chapter 11, "Impressions and Expressions") and must produce itself.

Many of us pay no attention to our motor element thoughts, but I urge you to take responsibility for them, because in doing so you take possession of the key to your freedom.

Scrutiny of reactions in times of triumph, fear, joy, or anger will tell us what the future holds in store for us.

Exercise

Every motor element thought will produce itself, requiring no special attention from us, unless we undo it. Practice daily the art of revising unwanted responses in the following way. In a comfortable, relaxed state, bring to mind an unwanted reaction to a particular event. Replay the scene as you wish it had occurred. Go over and over this imagined reaction until it takes on the tones of reality (Chapter 9, "The Human Body and Metaphysics"). When you have achieved satisfaction, you have succeeded in undoing the motor element thought and are now free from its potential effects.

We all place far too much emphasis on the conditions of life as the cause of our emotional state. It is our emotional state that is responsible for the conditions of our lives.

CHAPTER 5

Changing the Past

THE ABILITY TO undo events, especially those that have caused us pain, is an attractive prospect, but the attainment of this ability requires courage. Not courage in practice per se, as the technique in and of itself is simple, but courage—boundless courage—in belief.

The Metaphysical approach to this topic is revision, the act of repealing events that have already occurred and appear to be rooted in fact. These events are replaced with the version you wish had taken place instead, which then become, in consciousness, your new reality.

Making this a daily practice will in time reveal in you an ability to achieve any objective. This is not to be taken lightly, as you will awaken within yourself an awareness, the nature of which is unlimited creative power.

If you wish to know how altering the seemingly unalterable past can affect your present and future, you must put this theory to the test.

Failure is the sleep, not the death, of success. Infinite alternatives to your present reality exist; it is simply a matter of coming into contact with the states of consciousness in which your successes live. If you continue to walk the path you are presently walking, you are free of the effects of any other state of consciousness and must limit yourself to where the path you walk may lead you.

Revision alters your course. It is a function purely of consciousness and is free of the contaminants of logic, reason, and will. It urges you to relinquish the operation of your daily life to your higher being, knowing that, once awake, there is no limit to what you will be able to achieve.

Exercise

In addition to adopting a relaxed, calm state, you must also take on an attitude of forgiveness. This is so that you can review your entire day without judgment. Consider yourself in your entirety and forgive yourself. This is not difficult to do; it requires an appreciation of yourself that you can achieve even if you are not used to doing so. Simply consider your entire being, body and mind, from head to toe, and feel thankful.

In this attitude, replay your day from the moment you woke up to the point at which you retired for the day. Do your best to recall as much detail as possible, but do not strain or exert any effort.

Think of all the interactions you have had, all the events, including details such as eating a meal or watching television. Nothing is exempt as long as you can recall it without effort. As you go through your day, stop at any event that was displeasing to you. Then rewrite the scene. Play the revised scene over and over again until you are satisfied that it feels real to you. It should be sufficiently real to your subconscious mind that there is no difference to you between the imagined scene and the remembered scene.

At this point you begin the review of your day again, this time replacing the unhappy event with the one you have now constructed in its place. You may rewrite as many scenes as you wish, but it is advisable in the beginning to alter one event at a time during the reviewing process.

Then, in a happy mood of accomplishment, allow yourself to drift off into sleep.

That which you have impressed upon consciousness will run ahead to confront you as an entirely new version of your own life, one that while being familiar to you is far better in terms of its quality. The course you were on will be changed and you will find yourself on the path you would have taken, were your imagined activity an objective reality.

In the state of sleep, we are as one who is dead and awaiting resurrection. When we awake each morning, following night after night of this activity of mental review, we are not just awakening physically but we are also stirring from the real sleep of the soul. The sleep of our consciousness.

Do not ask how your resurrection will occur, neither be concerned with how long the process may take; only know that with the practice of revision this change must happen. It is a promise made to every living being. Our memories will slowly return and we will discover the true purpose of our life's journey undertaken by the being housed within us.

Fame and fortune are your right, all the pleasures this life affords are accessible to you, and there is nothing wrong in having these things. However, there are greater treasures awaiting the one who feels a deep, resonating hunger in the depth of themselves.

CHAPTER 6

An End to Suffering

THE BIBLICAL EDICT that Christ "daily bears our burdens" is for most people almost impossible to fully understand. Whether you are inclined to accept the existence of Christ or not, complications arise simply because the word *Christ* automatically conjures up an image of one separate from one's self. And if that is the case, the idea of Christ (ostensibly another being) feeling what we feel—or bearing our burdens on our behalf—becomes difficult to accept in practical terms.

The fact is, Christ is not a man. There was never a being that ever existed called Christ or Jesus Christ. The one talked about in the Bible who "takes our infirmities and bears our diseases" is your own human imagination—which is God himself.

Christ's teachings, together with those of other biblical characters and scriptural interpretation, are taught as
part of the core esoteric mysteries of Metaphysics, and it
is essential that every man and woman discovers the
truth for him- or herself. Until this discovery is made, the
Bible and its purpose as a psychological document will
make absolutely no sense.

For now, though, let us set aside the argument for non-
historicity of the Bible and consider how we might put an
end to suffering by Metaphysical means.

We must start with the crucifixion, which pertains to
the union between God and man. The crucifixion—
symbolized as Christ nailed to the cross—does require revelation, but ostensibly provides that humanity cannot be
separate from consciousness, which is causation. Christ, as
we have already established, is God or consciousness, while
the cross represents man (human beings).

For those schooled in religious doctrine, do not be distracted by what you have been taught about the crucifixion. It never occurred. The symbolism states only that at
the beginning of creation, at the commencement of God as
man on Earth, humanity and consciousness were joined
together.

To reassure you, in the Hebraic language the letter *VAU*,
which appears as the third letter in the name of God,
means "nail." According to ancient teaching, the purpose

of the nail is to bind two things together. Hence, Christ is bound to the cross (man) with the nail. You are free to study this subject further; however, I hope you will take my word for it, for now. Consciousness is God—human imagination—and God and man are one.

Once you are able to accept that God and man are one, try to think of yourself as God (Chapter 22, "You Are I Am"). What this then means is that whenever you refer to yourself, you are referring to God. A statement such as *I am happy* becomes *God is happy*. I am angry, God is angry. I am sick, God is sick, and so on.

Since your I Am is God, when you declare yourself to suffer, to be in pain, to have been wronged, are you not saying that Christ is suffering?

What we say of ourselves, we are saying of consciousness, for consciousness will always represent that which we accept as true with feeling. And this is the case for everyone, whether it is known or not.

As we go through life observing the horrors, we often become intimidated by them, and by reacting with feeling, we are bound to encounter these horrors in their various forms in the future. We feed the emotions of fear and anger and hatred and frustration by reacting to the evidence presented to us daily in a thousand ways, be it from the news media, the actions and words of others, or our own experiences.

We impress our fears upon consciousness and our fears become things, they become the monsters we must face, and they form the basis of our suffering.

But we are here for one purpose and one purpose only, and that is to fulfill God's plan for man, beginning with the crucifixion and ending with the resurrection.

The fact that creation is infinite and there are no limits to the ways in which we can express ourselves changes nothing. Human beings are merely unaware that they are asleep, awaiting resurrection. Even the vilest emanations from the most despicable human beings, which are also forms of expression, cannot be separated from God.

Man as God can and will be redeemed, which means that we can forgive anyone for the things that they do; it is the same God that operates in all of us.

> See now that I myself am he! There is no god
> besides me. I put to death and I bring to life, I
> have wounded and I will heal, and no one can
> deliver out of my hand.
> —Deuteronomy 32:39, *King James Version*

So, you see, there is no extra source of evil in the world responsible for all the pain and suffering, while God exists for all the good. There is only man and conscious-ness, which must pass through the furnaces of life together, for purification, for a rebirth, and only we can save ourselves.

Exercise

God is not in man, God became man—actually became man, so that man can reawaken as God. I fully comprehend that this may be the most outlandish thing you have ever heard, but I assure you that acceptance of this concept holds the key to ending your suffering. If you are going through some unspeakable pain at this moment, I invite you to open yourself to the following process.

Lying flat on your back with your head on the same level as your body (no pillow), and if possible completely undisturbed, begin to speak to yourself feelingly. If you are able to lie on the floor comfortably, you will find this most valuable during the process. You will be conversing with yourself as though you are two people, asking a question and then answering it.

Begin by asking, "Are you really God?" Pause, then answer, "Yes." Next ask, "Is it really true?" Pause, and answer, "Yes." Then ask, "What is your name?" Pause, and answer, "I Am." You may wish to wait a moment or two before continuing. Allow yourself to slip into the depth of yourself.

If you feel peculiar, don't be afraid; allow the feeling of expansion that comes on you to grow as you move deeper into consciousness. Ask, "Do you suffer as I suffer?" Answer, "Yes." Wait, and ask, "Do you feel the pain/sorrow/hurt (etc.) of _____?" Answer, "Yes." Then say, "Prove it to me now." You may feel heady, but don't be alarmed. You are transferring the sensation from your physical self to your consciousness, which is infinite and therefore allows the feeling to dissipate as it loses its structure and context.

As you let go of the emotion you are experiencing, continue to feel yourself to be "I Am." If you wish, you may choose to qualify the feeling. You may say,

I AM I heal, I AM I love, I AM I make alive, I AM I make the crooked paths straight, etc. Whatever you wish.

If you are presently going through a challenging period, it may be difficult to do this exercise in the moment, but be courageous; don't force yourself, but be willing to give it a try. You may feel uncomfortable when you return to the surface, but the sensation will pass once you have successfully cast the burden upon your higher self.

It may be difficult for you to believe in this process, particularly if you feel unready to stand on your own two feet, or if you find yourself unable to stop yourself blaming others for what happens to you. Perhaps you are facing too much turmoil at the moment. But I know that we are all required to address God as self in order to activate our innate authority over the darkness in the world.

All things have a purpose, as do all people, even the dreadful, deceitful, and terrible ones. Think of everyone as existing in a state of consciousness either wittingly or unwittingly. We are all playing our individual roles in the great universal performance of life. And, just as any actor can, we are free to pick and choose our parts.

If you can do this you will limit your pain, because you will understand that the one who causes the hurt is God, and as such every offender can be forgiven. Suffering has its place; it precedes perfection. By suffering we are made to seek and find the savior, who resides within. Do not be offended by this notion, neither try to force yourself to accept it. The degree to which this or any Metaphysical principle disturbs you depends on how deeply God is hidden in you. Approach this theory with a mind that is absolutely determined to put it to the test and it will not fail you.

If your loved one dies or some horrible calamity befalls you, if you give birth to a disabled child or witness some dreadful tragedy, do not for one moment entertain the idea that you are somehow at fault. You are being prepared, as we all are, for the end.

While we are here, let us cast the burden of our sufferings upon our true self, our higher being. This action serves a specific divine purpose, which is the discovery of the identity bestowed on us before birth.

CHAPTER 7

The Psychic Sexual Act

F EW PLEASURES IN LIFE compare to that of the physical creative act, the climax of which is an unmistakable feeling of relief that resonates, and in the process of
bringing our imaginative activities to life, we are able to
replicate this creative act in consciousness.

This is an incredibly effective and highly rewarding
method of making your desires an objective reality, and
here is how it is done.

Exercise

You must be mentally pliable and receptive in order

for this method to be effective. Relax by imagining

yourself as being, doing, or possessing the thing you

want. Feel good in your body, contemplate enjoying what you are about to do, as you bring your focus to rest on the feeling of possession.

As you experience your desire in imagination, breathe in and out in a rhythmic sensual manner. For this reason it is best if you are alone and undisturbed. As you breathe in and out, you should be aware of a pleasurable thrill or tremor that runs the course of your body. You should feel a tingling in your creative organ. Continue to breathe in and out, allow the sensation to build. Resist the sensation to caress yourself should the need arise.

You are consummating your desire in consciousness and the intensity of the thrill passing through your body will build just as the natural sensation would.

Then, at the peak of intensity, take one last deep, deep inhalation and allow yourself to release. It will occur as an explosion of power that closely mirrors the normal expected physical response. Do not be alarmed.

You have just performed a spiritual sexual act and you are now pregnant. Open your eyes, respond in the most natural, normal way for you; it is an entirely personal thing, but be confident, and rest assured that you must give birth to the physical manifestation of your desire.

As doubt is the only thing capable of causing a collapse of that which you have just established, be secretive. Tell absolutely no one of what you have done, so that you can pass through the necessary interval until your desire becomes a reality.

This act is the symbolic Immaculate Conception. You have achieved, without a man, the birth of your spiritual child; your desire has become a reality.

This event applies to all people regardless of gender—it uses the symbolism of natural conception, but the spiritual principle is universal.

Your desire will express itself as part of your new concept of self. It always happens this way, because you start living in the same state of consciousness as your desire in its fully formed condition. If you want to express the things you desire, you must reside in the state where these things live, so that you can interact with them in a normal, natural way. If a thing does not feel natural to you, as natural as any present element of your life, you cannot truly experience it.

CHAPTER 8

Subjective Control

THERE CANNOT BE too much emphasis placed upon the importance of attention and its control. If you are able to control the direction of your attention in the use of imagination, you will quickly discover your ability in the creative use of imagination to be an infallible, life-transforming power. It is the attention we give to something in mind that is the life force of the thing considered. We kill off those things we no longer wish to see or experience in our world by taking our attention away from them.

Attention is drawn either inwardly or outwardly, and in the world of Metaphysical mastery, it is our inward attention (subjective attention) that is most significant and in need of cultivation.

That which attracts from without is merely concerned with the immediate physical present; but the inward, the subjective, enables us to give life to a thing at any point in space or time, by making that which we are focused on (with the requisite intensity) an immediate fact.

During the waking phase of our day-to-day lives, we are oblivious to the effects of our subjective attention. This is because we are always preoccupied with our immediate physical reality, under a constant barrage of external stimuli. Additionally, developing control over the direction of our attention as pertains to the subjective will expose the vast difference between our objective and subjective experiences.

What follows is an invitation to take in hand the development of your internal focus, which will furnish you with both the ability and capacity to change your future.

It makes reasonable sense to suggest that the degree to which you are able to direct your attention subjectively is the degree to which your objective propensity is lessened.

In other words, as you concentrate on your emotions, your thoughts, and your moods (cherry-picking those that pertain to what you want to express), the things that you find limiting will fall away. Total control over the movement of your mind within the subjective field hands you mastery of your fate.

The exercises laid out in this book are deliberately

sequenced to lead you in the direction of a most supreme discovery: that God, or Christ, in you *is* you, as your own imagination.

This is a mystery that persists century after century and is awaiting revelation in all of us through experimentation and experience. It tells you that if God is all, and you are God, all things are under your control. This is a fact.

Exercise

One way to know whether you have dominance is to examine your relationship to others. For, how can we know that we are in divine control of inanimate things, or the conditions and circumstances of our lives? Our own prejudices, fears, beliefs, wishes, and suspicions may cloud our judgment and cause us to misinterpret an event.

There is no such ambiguity when it comes to the actions of another. If we are able to direct the behavior of a friend, have we not exerted preeminence?

Do not be alarmed at this thought. We are all one. Those who seem to be other than ourselves are just another aspect of us, just as we are another aspect of them. That which you can do to another can be done to you. In fact, the only way to protect yourself from harm is to relieve yourself of the ability to harm others. So the influence I am about to explain to you I pray will only be used for good.

Here is how you do it.

In order to link yourself with another person, you must be in a carefully thoughtful frame of mind, by which I mean, one in which your attention is fully withdrawn from the objective world around you. Close your eyes, and do not listen for external sounds or feel after your surroundings.

Think of the person you wish to contact mentally. Fix your attention on them—you may like to see them positioned in space somewhere in front of you, perhaps walking with their back to you.

Once you have located the person, call their name. Imagine yourself shouting as loudly as you can. All this must be done subjectively. If you feel your eyes moving behind their closed lids or feel the muscles of your mouth and/or throat responding to your imagined call, you are slipping into the objective. Pause and try again.

Imagine that the person you are calling stops walking and turns around, having heard your voice.

As you come together, you will have a conversation. The person you have identified will be saying exactly what it is you want them to say, confirming that everything you wish to see in your physical reality is now done. To fully immerse, you may wish to embrace the person, notice their smell, the feel of their body in yours, the sound of their voice close to your ear, their breathing, the texture of their clothes.

You should also note that if you can see your own face, you have not gone deep enough. Just as is the physical case, when we are talking to others we may see their faces but certainly not our own. If you are truly looking through your subjective eyes, you will not be able to see your own face.

You can achieve this level of expansion with a sustained inward focus. The moment you allow your mind to wander, the "spell" is broken.

Do not be alarmed; with practice and in time, the process will be effortless.

As the conversation goes on, be aware of your breathing, which should be as described in Chapter 7; a physical eruption is confirmation that your imagined activity has been successful.

You may now return to your objective reality.

You can by all means use this technique to reverse decisions that have gone against you and appear to be final, you may use it to secure a position, or acquire something that you need when the odds seem stacked against you, but I urge you not to use this ability to "get" people to do things such as giving you money. If you do, you will give way to tyranny, and it will backfire.

The destabilizing power of doubt is not to be underestimated. For this reason, it is important that you really immerse yourself in the process, rather than act as a spectator. Try not to let your mind entertain thoughts of skepticism while you are trying to make contact.

Achieving discipline in this practice will awaken in you spiritual knowledge that will in turn serve to quell the doubts and fears that blight you.

CHAPTER 9

The Human Body
and Metaphysics

THERE ARE BILLIONS of people in the world, all separate yet bound by one unifying thing: it is not our
functionality but the nature of consciousness that makes
us all the same.

Our physical bodies typify the experience of God indi-
vidualized as man, the Elohim (God as many sons). What
this means in Metaphysical terms is that, while the forms
of our physical bodies differ from each other in appear-
ance, the forms of our individual bodies are identical to
our spiritual ones.

Exercise

Let's now turn our attention to the means by which we experience the world around us—via our five senses—and develop the habit of switching between the senses we possess bodily and those we possess in consciousness.

Our aim is to reach the required level of natural-ness whenever we are using our imagination cre-atively. That is the only way to bring your thoughts quite literally to life.

Try this simple exercise as often as you like. In a relaxed, happy state, hold an object in your physical hand. If it has a distinct odor or taste, you may wish to smell and taste the object. Experience the item as fully as you can. Then put it down, close your eyes, and take the object in your subjective hand (imagine holding the object). It is important that you do not visualize yourself doing this but feel that you have an invisible hand and it is holding something distinct. If need be, taste and smell the object as before, only this time using your subjective senses. Continue to do this until you feel the object is real.

If you wish to know whether you are truly operating in the subjective, check to see if you are seeing the world clearly behind your closed lids. You will notice that you cannot see your face apart from the bridge of your nose or the curve of your cheeks. You will have the same first-person perspective as you would in real life.

This technique is simple but requires practice.

One of the greatest and most valuable scientific discoveries made about the human body is the connection between physical ailments and the psyche. Problems that arise from stress, or emotional issues like depression and anxiety, are common knowledge, and their treatment often involves some form of prescribed relaxation or de-stressing.

When we fail to relax we experience pain because

our minds are not at rest, but when we are asleep we feel nothing because we have relinquished control over the things around us. The business of going about our daily business is mostly an effort of will.

For this reason, we are taught in Metaphysics to relax as deeply as possible whenever we are exercising our imagination creatively. In fact, a condition bordering on sleep is most effective in bringing about our aims.

Ultimately the Metaphysical student is working toward entering at will into a physical state of attention without effort governed by the subjective mind.

CHAPTER 10

Metanoia

METANOIA, OR REPENTANCE, is the secret to changing your world by first changing your attitude toward it. It is a penetrative understanding that any attempt to alter your reality without this inward change is fruitless and an anathema to the Law of Creation.

Everyone in the world is facing some horror or other, and those horrors, being just as rooted in our imaginal activity as all the good we would pursue, are just as capable of producing their correlative physical effects.

We're all accustomed to pointing the finger, but metanoia, as referenced by the ancients, determines that we travel inward and do not stop until we reach the source, the point at which we think of ourselves as I Am. This inflection is repentance, because we must, in order to see

God, forgive all of mankind and take full responsibility for the world in which we live, the world that I Am as the creator has made.

As we repent, we begin to tear down the structures that we unwittingly built, by placing our attention on what we want to see instead, bearing in mind that to the extent you are persuaded that this is so, it will be the case.

Until we take authority over ourselves, we are subject to external influences and the creations of a wild and un-fettered imagination. Some may find themselves doing unspeakable things without explanation, while others, through the process of unchecked fear and negative think-ing, may find wonderful things disappearing from their lives.

As tempting as it may seem to be able to lay the blame for our misfortunes at the feet of another, we must be willing to give this up in order to become free.

Exercise

You will learn by this very simple method how not to take no for an answer.

Bring to mind something you wish to change. Emo-tions such as anger or frustration are not a hindrance;

in fact, you can operate through any emotion if it is inextricably linked to the matter at hand. Enter the emotion by noticing it, and thinking about those elements of the circumstance that gave rise to it. Catch the emotion, and you will give the thing you want to change subjective reality.

Now, operating in the subjective, you will move to contact the emotion associated with the situation as you want it to be. Reach for the emotion you would experience if the circumstance were as you wished it to be. If this is confusing, think of being happy for no particular reason. In other words, imagine that you feel good but cannot place your finger on what it is exactly that is making you feel that way.

This is far easier than it seems, as you will discover once you start to experiment with this idea.

Remember, all things in the subjective world are an immediate fact. Hold the *emotion* associated with the desired state and, just as you gave your present circumstance subjective reality, you will also give your desired state subjective reality.

In order to see the result of this exercise take on physical form, sustain this emotional state to the point of eruption. This is the quickest and most certain way. You can liken this surge of power to the exposure of a photographic negative that will shortly thereafter bring into view a clear picture.

CHAPTER 11

Impressions and Expressions

WE COMMUNICATE WITH the subjective world in one way only, through the language of feeling, and God—human imagination—communicates with us through the language of desires. Our desires are always relative to our present state of consciousness and are crafted to inspire an ascension through their fulfillment.

One who is in ill health desires good health, one who is poor desires wealth, one who feels themselves unknown desires fame, and on it goes.

Everyone believes their desires to be myogenic, self-inspired, or the product of some external source of influence; but they are God in action, moving us ever upward through the cycle of dissatisfaction, desire, and fulfillment.

The things we crave, once we have them, quickly lose their capacity to satisfy, and we must move on to bigger and better things.

Without this quality of man, none of us would progress, and all humans would stagnate and die. If we are not moving forward we are dying, for death is the opposite of life, which God is, in absolute terms. Life is known by the ability of a living thing to move forward, propelled along a time sequence under the guidance of an extra-existential force—that is to say, the ability that living thing has to exist from one moment to the next.

So then, God impresses upon us his desires for himself, that which he wishes to see expressed in this world, and we respond by impressing upon consciousness with feeling the things we want.

This doesn't mean that we don't have a role to play in our own creative function; the statement that God desires in us is substantive. We are given absolute free rein to choose which state of consciousness we would occupy, but it is God in all, as all that makes our desires is divine will.

Once we are able to feel strongly enough about anything, sufficiently so that an impression is made, the thing we have impressed must in turn be expressed as a physical fact in our present reality.

Exercise

Here we practice focusing our attention on the intensity of our feelings for the purpose of using at will this divine gift in a consciously creative manner. We need not give this method a dry run, but can dive right in at the deep end. What do you want? Define it as clearly as you can, in as vivid detail as you can. Do not rush this process but spend time, enjoying laying an intricate foundation. You may even wish to position your desire at a specific time in a specific location. (If you want to do this, however, you must first fix the time-space condition psychologically and self-persuade yourself of the reality of what you are now seeing, hearing, doing, etc.)

You will now practice altering the intensity of your feeling (the feeling you're in possession of now) as though adjusting the focus on a lens.

Sharpen the intensity of feeling by a deliberate and determined concentration, a hard focus, if you will, then soften it by allowing your attention to drop.

Think in terms of how you are able to bring different objects arranged spatially in and out of focus by minute movements of the muscles of the eye. Treat your feeling like a muscle that you can contract and relax at will.

With practice you will be able to manipulate this action as easily as you breathe.

An intense focus will always make an impression, and once an impression is made you will be in no doubt as to this being the case. For confirmation, observe the following phenomena: an intensely dry mouth and/or dry hands; a pale blue shade, albeit a crisp, transparent one, resting over your field of vision—this lasts from a few moments to several minutes and is like looking through a colored lens. Clusters of cells, unmistakably red blood cells dancing before your eyes. We are all used to seeing little

black squiggles or dots on occasion, but these are
unmistakably blood cells.

You then wait with patience for the short interval
to elapse until you reap the fruit of your mental activity.

This technique will likely suit the temperament of those
who prefer not to experience a sensation that resembles a
sexual climax. As with all the exercises outlined in this
book, feel free to modify in any way you wish, as long as
you stick to the pattern of the instruction as laid out.

=

CHAPTER 12

Fantasize with Focus

O NE OF THE things that will make the practice of Metaphysics easier is acceptance of its guiding principles to such an extent that they become an integral part of your way of thinking.

You are not being asked to take anything at face value, but you are being asked to accept the structure of these principles in the way one might accept the structure of the law of gravity. As with other theories, you are then free to put those of Metaphysics to the test, in essence to prove the truth of the ideas put forward for yourself by testing them through experimentation.

The principle we are concerned with here teaches that all things already exist and that it is impossible to be aware of something that does not exist on some level.

Taking this one step further, we know from Metaphysics that anything you are aware of can be experienced as "real" while in a deep relaxed state of what I call mental play or reverie; that's to say you can use your imaginal or subjective senses to experience the reality of a thing.

Let's turn, then, to the practice of making our reverie a productive, focused form of daydreaming for the purpose of acquiring the things we would most like to possess.

Exercise

You will be calling into existence a constructed scene by entering into it through imagination. All states of consciousness lie dormant waiting for an occupant to imbue them with life force. Metaphorically, entering into a particular state of consciousness is like walking into a fully functional and furnished building that is still and quiet through lack of use. Once the power is turned on, there is light and sound and movement. Everything in the building is plain to see and can be experienced.

In consciousness, as you draw close to a particular state, you will be aware of what resembles a set scene draped in darkness. You will know that you have entered the state once the scene is bathed in light and color.

As this is daydreaming with purpose, you will fully immerse yourself into the scene you have constructed. While you can allow your mind to wander, the mental paths you take must be associational. That's to say, you can imagine yourself in a new job or owning a home, but all associated thoughts must pertain to the reality of this being the case. Don't jump from being in a new job to performing onstage if there is no logical link between the two.

In this way you control the direction of your attention.

You may engage in this activity for as long or short a period as you wish, but endeavor to imaginatively experience the physicality of what you are seeing.

Do away with all of the limiting ideas you hold about God; discard, with absolute confidence, the ideas showered down on us from pulpits and other religious edifices. God is pure imagination working at the core of every human being, underlying every conceivable faculty.

We have heard over and over again, "It's only your imagination," but imagination is God, the source of all that exists, and until you begin to earnestly question and seek after imagination, you can never fully understand the significance or power of this fact.

Imagination is unfettered spiritual sensation and can be used by you proportionally to the extent that you test it. You test it by feeling after things that are not presently physically evident.

If I ask you to sense (imagine) a rose, to feel its soft petals or perceive its delicate fragrance, or I ask you to mentally experience the biting astringency of a lemon, or handle a golf ball, taking in its distinct dimpled form, you would be able to tell me that they are all different. The fact that they feel, smell, or taste differently, even in imagination, means they must exist.

So, develop the habit of sensing things, believe in the reality of what you are feeling, and your faith will bring the invisible and intangible into view.

Start small, if that helps; give yourself a new car, a new job, a new home, greater income, vibrant health—you will soon grow hungry for greater things such as clairvoyance, using your newly discovered ability to assist others, or the ability to interpret the bible and other spiritual documents. We have all been given the freedom to do and have what we choose. Make as many mistakes as are necessary; all men stumble in the dark. It is your willingness to invoke the gift buried in you that matters.

Move past your belief in a world that is limited to what your five senses tell you it is. Nothing is unchangeable— even those things that seem way beyond your control. But I urge you to leave the world alone; if you have not been "sent," don't go. Concentrate on yourself and your relationship to the world you personally live in.

The world is a schoolroom and we have not been sent to change it, but rather to change ourselves.

CHAPTER 13

Success

WHEN YOU BELIEVE that what you are imagining is true, you are guaranteeing your success in bringing what you imagine into physical view. There is no limit to your capacity for belief, but it cannot be reasonably asserted without proof. The only way to prove to yourself that God as imagination makes things that are not seen, seen, is to put your imagination to the test.

Don't depend only on what you see with your physical eyes or what you hear or feel, but persist in the knowledge that whatever you have experienced subjectively has the potential to become real and will certainly become real using any of the methods outlined in this book.

There are other occultic secrets that you can become privy to once a certain level of experience has been achieved.

The principal of these is that of evoking a central vortex of power via a variation on the practice of revision. Without holding too much back, I urge you to have a very serious mind whenever you approach any of the techniques in this book; it is the surest and safest way of learning deeper mysteries and will come with the added benefit of experience. In this way no one is merely trying to indoctrinate or influence you.

Once you know the truth of a thing for yourself, external opinions are essentially meaningless and you eliminate the effect of miscommunication.

Even if you feel your knowledge at this point is restrictive, getting into the habit of persisting in the belief of your imaginal activity to the point of physical reality will trigger a series of psychological (spiritual) events, and what you feel is presently not known to you will become known to you.

Let me remind you to keep your objectives secret. The Bible instructs, "Go, tell no man." It is an essential rule.

That which you have contacted in imagination will become real to you as an objective fact in your life, but arrival may be delayed if you allow yourself to become doubtful. There is no easier route to doubt than through the words and actions of others. A smirk, a raising of the eyebrows, a barbed comment. Pay no attention to what other people think, and help yourself by keeping your aims hidden from them.

Success is a state of consciousness that must be worn at all times. It is entirely possible to occupy more than one psychological state at a time. If you feel yourself to be successful, you will achieve success in your Metaphysical endeavors, just as you will in all other aspects of your life.

Exercise

To take on the psychological state of success, formulate a phrase that implies you are successful. This is not to be confused with an affirmation such as, "I earn one hundred thousand dollars a year," but a statement of not more than three words that sums up your own sense of success. You will need to think about the words you will use. You may be inspired by another person, but the phrase you decide upon should only relate to you.

Repeat the phrase to yourself over and over. Not in a robotic fashion, but feelingly, which means considering each word and noticing how you feel when you use it. If you do not experience any registerable sensation, change the words. Depending upon how often you repeat the phrase, you will soon become possessed by its power.

What you inwardly tell yourself is of paramount importance and is the crux of the great secret of success. All successful people will tell you that, for them, positive thoughts relative to self are second nature. It is impossible for someone who condemns him- or herself to have success.

Because you are keeping your inner conversations hidden, you can be unrelenting in your self-adulation. Unashamedly extol yourself and the virtues you possess. What you say of yourself you are saying of God. Glorify God by glorifying yourself.

There is no great sacrifice required other than giving up your former thought patterns.

CHAPTER 14

Failure

I WOULD BE DERELICT in my duty if I did not address the issue of failure in the process of creative manifestation.

Thankfully, there is one cause and one only for failure in any effort you make to bring your imaginative work into being, and that is failure to persist to the point of physical reality.

When you are pursuing something in imagination, you are not asked to think about it once or twice and let it go, hoping for the best. You are asked to experience the reality of the thing sought and persist in this experience until there is no discernible difference between that which you are imagining and its correlate were the thing already a physical reality.

We are taught that at the point of naturalness (a phrase often used by Neville to mean the point at which a thing that is imagined and a thing that physically exists are indistinguishable from each other) that which was imagined has become real.

When you experience your desire using your subjective senses, your sensation may seem vague; repeating the action will cause the sensation to intensify. At some point, when the sensation is strong enough, it will have crystallized. In other words, it will have become a physical thing.

This crystallization is not separate from the original imaged idea; it is simply the idea in another form, at another point along the timeline of its existence.

All things were first imagined.

Persist in the reality of your imaginal activity by experiencing it subjectively until it takes on a life of its own.

Exercise

Practice with feeling, imagining, a golf ball rolling around in your palm, or the feeling of some other distinct object in your hand. Hold the object and feel its firmness, feel its texture, while telling yourself that the imagined feeling is a real physical sensation. It could take you a few moments or several weeks, depending on the intensity of your self-persuasion. No matter how long this takes, sooner or later the item will take on the feeling of reality.

Once you have developed your sense of touch in this way, you will find manifesting your desires to be an effortless pleasure.

With something you desire, do not relent at the point of sensation. Continue to experience your desire as though it were true, and it will become true. What this means is that you continue to react to your desire as though it were already a visible fact. You do not need to be quiet or still to do this, you could be anywhere doing anything—just direct your attention to notice your desire in its fulfilled state. Experience the emotions that your attention evokes not as happy or comforting feelings of something on the way, but as celebratory feelings of the thing you want being real. You should maintain these feelings

until the invisible has become visible.

The surge of power you feel when your imaginal activity has been successful is not the end of the story. This is just confirmation that what you have done has worked and will go ahead to meet you in the very near future. But do not be concerned with when.

If you are going about your daily business as though what you have desired is already a fact, you may not even notice the point at which fantasy becomes reality.

CHAPTER 15

—

Believing the Unbelievable

THERE ARE NO limits to what you can imagine and bring about in your world, if you believe. You already have a set of beliefs some of which may be very strongly held indeed, but are you willing to reach beyond them and move into the realm of belief that logic and reason pour scorn on?

If you are, you will break through the limiting barriers of reasonableness into a life of unlimited possibilities, where all things exist and are accessible to you.

The choice is yours; you can, at will and at any moment, operate from the premise that the source of all creation dwells and works in you as your own imagination.

"With God all things are possible" is a familiar refrain, but many find it unacceptable that all things are possible to man. Why? Because many as yet fail to accept that God and man are one.

If you are loath to regard God as anything other than a foreboding supreme deity, or are as yet unwilling to regard the existence of God at all (and I hope that you are not), you will find it difficult to use your imagination in a consciously creative way. Your life will remain as it is and you will be stuck walking laps until you are ready to end this particular journey—only to find yourself back in the journey again, oblivious to what and who you have left behind, and needing to proceed once more.

However, when you can see that you and God (human imagination) are one, you will begin at once to live a meaningful, magnificent life.

If you could change your daily experience, uprooting the unpleasant things and planting lovely things in their place, wouldn't you? If you could heal relationships or transform the lives of those you love without struggling to find solutions to seemingly unsolvable problems, wouldn't you?

Reason dictates that life as you presently understand it should be managed and put up with. You know your bank balance, the level of your education, the state of your health, and the condition of your relationships, and there is nothing to suggest that things can be altered outside the parameters of any proffered help.

But believe that your imagination is the source of life, and you blow your personal situation wide open. Be self-persuaded. Convince yourself that it is indeed true that all things are first imagined and that whatever you imagine is also true. Do this, and you are giving yourself the power to soar beyond the confines of reason.

You may believe in your employment, but if your employment is not sufficient to meet your financial needs, imagine you have received an increase in salary. Live as though it were true by failing to notice feelings of insecurity or anxiety. If you dare to focus your attention on feelings of security and betterment in the midst of what you are going through, you will be surprised by how things change.

Use whatever technique speaks to you in moments of concern.

Exercise

Just before you drift off to sleep, empty your mind of the thoughts that disturb you and ask how you would feel if the thing you most desire were true. Spend a little time relaxing. If your mind is too busy with thoughts from the day or with pressing issues, wait until you feel sufficiently sleepy. You will be making a concerted effort not to drift off into sleep in a state of unrest or panic. If you do, you are setting yourself up to face the same problems tomorrow.

Instead, allow yourself a little time dedicated to you. Tell yourself that there is no harm in setting aside your concerns for the time being (if that helps). Remind yourself that there is nothing you can do to address things just as you are about to sleep.

For example, if you need money, ask yourself how you would feel if you had money. You are not referencing the things you need money for, but solely focusing on what your life with money would look and feel like.

Remember, do not say something like, "I would pay off my credit cards," and imagine yourself doing so, but think in terms of, "I would treat myself to a new car," and imagine yourself doing just that.

Notice the pleasant, pleasurable sensation that arises in response to this, and hold your attention on it as you drift off to sleep. I don't now know how many nights it will take for your activity to bear fruit, but I do know that the intensity of focus and the feeling of reality (naturalness) will reduce the time you have to wait.

God and human imagination are identical, and the equating of yourself with God is a most sensible practice. If you are already some way toward believing that all things are possible to God, and you are able to identify your true relationship to God, you will grow in confidence, believing all things to be possible to you.

CHAPTER 16

The Invisible World You Live In

WHILE WE SEE with our objective vision, we are blind to the subjective. Similarly, it is by closing off our objective vision that we are able to view things subjectively.

To develop your faculty of subjective vision, routinely engage in the following practice.

EXERCISE

Sitting quietly in a room, draw your attention away from your surroundings. Attempt to do this with your eyes open. Soften your focus by placing your attention on something you know well that is located in another room. For example, you may be sitting in your living room or kitchen and ignoring the table or chairs or television; now rest your attention on—that is to say, mentally look at—your bed in your bedroom, or, if you feel able to, look through the window of that room.

Do not force yourself to see, but allow yourself to see. This is not quite the same as remembering what you are looking at, but if you must, use your memory to aid you at first.

You may begin to feel a sensation of strain behind your eyes. If this happens, close your eyes and try again.

This will feel uncomfortable until you are used to it, because your subconscious mind is struggling against the fact that you are seeing what it is you only think you are seeing.

Return to your present surroundings by looking at the environment around you, and then repeat the process.

I leave it to you to decide how long to continue.

Do not overdo it. If you have a headache, feel a little discomfort in your chest, or feel woozy, wait a day or so before trying again. You will find that your resistance to what is occurring is the cause of your physical distress. Concentrated attention trained in a particular direction shuts out everything else. You will find that as you are focused on the item not in your immediate physical presence, you will be unable to think of anything else.

When it comes to manifesting the things we want, we should be confident to explore all the things we don't want by this same method of concentrated attention.

This exercise develops our innate spiritual sight and enables us to penetrate into the fourth dimension, the realm of consciousness. A little practice will soon convince you of that.

That which holds our attention compels us to act in

uniformity with its being, and our actions seem to be the most natural thing in the world from this premise.

Our desires come in the form of something we desire to be, do, or have in order to make our lives better somehow, more pleasurable, and none of these are unselfish, even those pertaining to others. But this is necessary. We must be selfish, completely selfish, so that we are unrelenting in our ambition to change the self. It is only by a transformation of self that we reveal our true identity.

All states of consciousness are invisible until we occupy them, but they are only invisible to our outer being. Let us then constantly contemplate the invisible, which is the world in which you as causation reside. Make a point of hearing with your invisible ears, tasting with your invisible tongue, feeling with your invisible hands, and seeing with your invisible eyes.

CHAPTER 17

Forging Your Social Status

Despite all evidence to the contrary, there is no system in place in the world of man capable of preventing you from occupying any position you wish to occupy, nor of your having any experience you wish to have. The basis of this claim is the instructional biblical edict, "No man cometh unto me unless I call him."

While it is far easier to point to an external source of help or misfortune than it is to turn inward and say, "I am solely responsible for my successes and failures," we are told in no uncertain terms that anyone we meet and the interactions that ensue only happen because the being that lies hidden within us draws them.

This is a hard thing to accept, no doubt about that, especially in light of overwhelming evidence to support the idea of others being in a position of dominance or subservience to us. But if you were not conscious of being disregarded, no one could disregard you, and if you were not conscious of being valued, no one could value you. This principle has not a thing to do with your physical background as you perceive it to be. Your background does not make you immune to the effects of a particular state of consciousness, nor does it make you prone to them.

While this truth may seem harsh to many, it is nevertheless the truth. As long as you remain in a particular state of consciousness, you are subject to the effects of it and untouched by the effects of another. We are given no authority to alter a state of consciousness; we may only give it life through occupancy. Change is achieved by psychological movement, which happens spiritually by the techniques outlined in this book. It's a bit like moving around your own home—your location in a particular room determines what you do when you get there; in the kitchen you might eat or cook, in the bedroom you'll likely sleep, while in the bathroom you'd brush your teeth. Mental states can similarly be described as locations, regions of the psyche or consciousness that determine how we behave once we get there.

When an inner being or higher self is referred to, few of us really know who it is. This is because we have never really taken the time to know who it is.

We are blissfully unaware that the embodiment of our imagination, our human consciousness having neither face nor form, molds itself into the shape of the thing we have impressed upon ourselves by our belief in that thing.

We may say we believe, but it often takes self-interrogation, an almost forensic scrutiny of mind, to know whether we truly believe that it is our own consciousness that forms the things around us.

The reason the truth of our feelings lies hidden from conscious perception is that they are buried under unnumbered emotional permutations, prejudices, and superstitions perpetuated by the condition of our environment. It is these qualities of consciousness that are projected outward, large as life, for all the world to see.

Certainly, we hold views about those different from ourselves, and when we see our perceptions acted out in the behaviors and circumstances of others we take this as confirmation—but it is only confirmation of what we believe and have thus occasioned to be the case. Why? Because what we see of another person is not the truth or a fact from their perspective, rather it is the truth or a fact from our own perspective.

What we must not fail to understand is that the infinite being is the one we really love. It is covered and kept safe inside of our physical bodies, it is all-powerful and is the sole architect of our fortunes and distresses. It is also solely responsible for what we personally see in the world. So when you read the words, "No man cometh unto me unless I call him," it is the inner being doing the calling.

Exercise

I hope that you will be self-persuaded that anyone who comes your way and fulfills a particular role does so under your divine instruction. The same applies to groups of individuals; no arrangement is exempt. Whether you see one person or an entire community of people as standing between where you presently are and where you wish to be, you can by a simple rearrangement of mind clear a path to your realized objective.

Try this. Suppose you wish to be a member of a particular society but feel that you are somehow not "in"—perhaps you are not from the right social background, the right racial background, the right economic background, the right whatever. Ignore these seeming obstacles and imagine you are being con-gratulated on your membership. Hear the voices welcoming you and listen as though hearing in space their words. You may also wish to feel a handshake. Take the subjective hand of the one welcoming you in your own subjective hand and keep shaking it, feeling as you do the telltale joyful thrill coursing through your body. Remain like this until you reach the point of eruption.

It is worth pointing out that it is perfectly accept-able to imagine those you know discussing your new position. They may be angry or envious, it does not matter. Hearing these words in your imagination will only add fuel to your fire.

Perhaps you wish to occupy a certain position within a company but feel you do not possess the necessary experience or qualifications. Again, apply this exact same principle.

You are not trying to win people over. Leave them alone and concentrate on yourself. If someone is

hateful or pessimistic, they are only hurting themselves. What I am saying is you will find that the
small-mindedness or the petty grievances of the
peevish and envious will not be a hindrance to you.
You will always be treated with dignity and respect
as long as you are conscious of being treated so.
People may not understand or like their sudden urge
to please you, but they will be powerless to resist.

God dwells in everyone, and is the only cause of all of the
phenomena of creation. If, after you have discovered this
to be true, you fail to act in bringing about the things you
want, you only have yourself to blame. Do not be in possession of such enormous power and hesitate for a moment to make use of it. Don't feel embarrassed or ashamed
of using your imagination to gain social position—and
remember, there is no need to tell anyone about what it is
you're trying to do. There is no shame in wanting things
in this life, it is God doing the desiring through you. Once
we satisfy our earthly hunger acquiring material posses-
sions or the acceptance and approval of others, we will

swiftly find them to be meaningless. Fulfillment of our desires is making room for our heavenly appetites.

The physical world around you tells you about the being within, the one whom you do not yet fully know. You could describe another person, a certain culture or society, but you are really describing yourself. You must accept this first before you attempt to change. Once you have accepted, it becomes so much easier to live in the world.

We will bless and curse not, and find our lives evolved into things of beauty, happiness, and success.

Do not for a moment concern yourself with how your objective will fulfill itself. If it takes a thousand men to bring it to pass, they will be directed and act accordingly. The influence is divine and brooks no resistance. You don't even need to know who might be involved; just know that God, who gave you the desire in the first place, has already provided the means. God is never in competition with himself. What he urges you and others to do has already been planned out in minute detail.

CHAPTER 18

———
——

Fearlessness

IMAGINATION IS BORN of love and because of this it is only through love that we know the truth about ourselves, things, and others. The truth that then frees us is knowledge of the identity of the thing considered. Nothing is hidden, and with absolute knowledge comes the elimination of fear.

If we imagine unlovingly, we deny ourselves the ability to lose our fears; our power is sent out in destructive directions, perverting and distorting the truth to create the horrors we face in the world.

To use your imagination unlovingly on behalf of self or others is to reduce yourself from a position of creative supremacy to that of pernicious mediary, bringing division between the unity of God and mankind.

Love creates. All things originate in love, no matter how insignificant they may appear, and the opposite effect of love is fear.

Love and fear have each been given the job of operating our mental faculties, and all that we see in the world around us was born of either of these two.

To live a truly fearless life even in the midst of all the terror in the world, we must cultivate the habit of thinking lovingly at all times. It is entirely possible to do.

Exercise

This is an exercise in training the imagination to pass all we do in thought through the filter of infinite love. Think of a person you know. Allow your mind to fill with everything you believe to be true about them. It will help if it is someone of whom you are not particularly fond. Do not judge them by calling to mind particular instances during which they have offended or upset you, just think about them as a human being. How do you feel about them? What sort of thing would you say about them? Once you are satisfied that you have answered the questions fully, ask yourself, "Would I accept this about me? Or would I accept this for me?"

If the answer is no, you must let those thoughts go. Cleanse yourself by imagining this same individual as you would like them to be. Wouldn't it be wonderful if so-and-so were kind or generous, or fun to be with? Stay with this new idea for a few moments, then embrace and hold the person until you feel unity with them. Carrying out a mental conversation with them, self-persuaded of the reality that they are saying things and acting the way you want them to.

Do the same for yourself, bring to mind the things you find to criticize yourself about. Ask, "Do I want to be like this?" Answer, "No," then rid yourself of these negative thoughts and emotions by immediately imagining yourself as you wish to be.

No matter how terrifying a person may be in real life, they are totally unaware of your imaginal activity relative to them and as such are in a hypnotic state in which you are able to make suggestions that they must follow. You are free to make them the gentlest, kindest, most thoughtful person you know.

If your fear is of something other than another person, repeat the same process, asking yourself whether the thing is as you want it to be or your behavior is as you want it to be. It does not matter what it is, the same principle applies. Hold the idea of yourself free of the fear and you will be.

Love is our birthplace, and as such we can never be separated from it. We can only act outside of love by entertaining negative and destructive thoughts. When we do that, we act in fear and must bear the consequences of our fears incarnated.

When the one housed within you is awakened, fear is defeated. Do not be afraid; this cannot not be emphasized strongly enough or often enough. Remember, when our mental faculties are operated by fear, our vision is distorted.

A bully cannot be a bully without the bullied. If you refuse to occupy the psychological state of one who is easily intimidated or bullied, all of the bullies in the world could band themselves together and they would find nothing in you and would be powerless. "The prince of this world cometh and finds nothing in me"—John 14:30.

CHAPTER 19

Perfect Self-Expression

God's divine plan for us is to make men perfect as he is perfect. After we have gone through all of the trials and tribulations of this life, like gold being purified in fire, we will awake from our present slumber to find our individuality replaced with the divine image, and without loss of identity.

Our present sleep is so deep we do not know that we are sleeping. It is in this state that we are called upon to be imitators of God as dear children, using our imagination to transform the invisible substance of consciousness into physical tangible things.

Because we are asleep, God is constantly disturbing us, urging us through the language of desire to prove his existence in us over and over again. If this were not so, we would be doomed to sleep forever.

Instead we find ourselves desiring increasingly grander things, better positions, greater wealth, better health, all inspired to move us upward and forward.

Don't be distracted by the hypnotic effects of life. Financial fluctuations, political uprisings, hostilities, famine, war, fame, fortune, material wealth—none of these things really mean anything. They will all be left one day.

Their purpose is mirroring to you what is lacking in you or the psychological movements that need to be made.

No matter the social policies passed, the community actions undertaken, anyone in a psychological state barring them from rescue will not be rescued. It is left to the individual to discover that no one other than oneself can feed their hunger, quench their thirst, clothe them, or give them shelter.

The world cannot and will not change, and there is not a thing you can do about it. You can give all you have to feed the hungry and clothe the naked, but anyone who persists in a psychological state of hunger and poverty will not be redeemed by your actions.

Now, if you feel inspired to do charitable work, by all means do so. It is a noble thing to help others and will do you good. But no amount of kindness can erase the states of destitution in this world, because all states of consciousness are permanent, available for anyone to occupy them at any time.

All things in this world have a purpose: to provide resistance against which every conceivable imaginal act of man can press. There can be no limit to the good, and neither to the bad, because imagination itself has no limit.

Exercise

In this exercise you will experience a most disconcerting sensation of expansion that may feel as if your body is being disjointed. Do not be afraid—you are not losing your mind, nor doing damage to your body. You must lie very quiet and still and take your attention away from your physical surroundings by closing your eyes and looking into the darkness behind your eyelids. Keep looking into the dark until you feel yourself slip into a peculiar form of relaxation.

In this state, begin to feel after infinite love. You could repeat the phrase "I Am" feelingly. It is entirely possible that you will find yourself in the depths of a great body of water—continue to breathe, don't panic. If you become aware of enormous bodies in the water around you, don't worry, they are the giants of the deep, they will do you no harm. Hear their voices, feel their heartbeats, unite with them as their creator. What comes next is an entirely individual thing—you may be aware of brilliant light or bright colors, fantastical shapes that make no sense that appear to be like giant jewels. Pass through all of these things, traveling further and further until you feel yourself ready to return.

When you wish to get back to objective reality, take your time. It is possible that you will feel as though you are stuck outside of your body and it may take a short time for physical sensation to return. Remember the bed you are lying on. In a short time feeling will return, first to your extremities, then moving inward, until you are fully restored to life.

The rewards of this process will be made known to you. No two individuals can experience this journey in the same way.

⑥

If you were to tell others about what you are doing they may laugh at you, some may even call you foolish or worse, but there is no need to tell anyone. Your purpose is only known through revelation, and revelation comes through a relationship with the being that resides within you. What is life without purpose anyway? If you owned all that the world has to offer and were the most famous, or the most physically attractive, but had no purpose, what good would any of those things do?

Set aside any trifling doubts, any notion of self-consciousness, and put the theories of Metaphysics to the test. God literally became man, complete with all of man's failing and limitations, so that man might know who he truly is.

CHAPTER 20

Perfect Health

THE IMPORTANCE OF good physical health cannot be overlooked. The desires that exist in your consciousness seeking embodiment require a body that is physically equipped for their fulfillment. Ill health is a distraction and a hindrance.

Your health should be recognized as something entirely within your power to control and subject to your imagination.

Pain and disease are the result of negative energies being held by the cells and tissues of the body. Whatever your physical symptoms may be, whatever damage has been done, do not forget that the underlying cause of all ailments is negative energy that needs to be released. When we speak about negative energy, we mean quite literally that. If the electrical charge of the energy held by your diseased cells were measured, that charge would be negative.

Negativity is an indication of instability and shares in common the destabilizing nature of the emotions that cause it.

You may have extensive knowledge about the molecular biology of the cells of the body, but whether you agree with my statements about negativity or not, this Metaphysical principle remains unchanged.

Negativity in the physical sense is a representation of negativity in the Metaphysical sense, and although we don't have the means to measure electrical energy in the spiritual sense, there is absolutely no difference between the two.

Negative energy is not only destructive, it is creative as well, and is capable of producing the most devastating effects.

Exercise

Your aim during this exercise is to bring about an agreement between yourself and the state of consciousness sought. Because of the nature of sickness, it is not always possible to hold your attention steady. If you are in excruciating pain you may be hard-pressed to treat the pain as though it were not there. In light of this, the following method provides an alternative route to the same objective, health and well-being in place of sickness and pain.

When pain is at its worst, resistance is at its peak and you are at your highest point of awareness. Specifically, you are acutely aware of being in a state of ill health.

While lying flat or sitting in a comfortable chair, enter into your consciousness via the medium of the discomfort you presently feel. Place your attention on the discomfort and hold it there. You may enter consciousness this way but should not dwell on this awareness. Immediately begin to tell yourself that you are "I Am." Do not mouth or speak aloud the words, just feel that you are the great creator, I Am. Relax and allow yourself to expand. You can quietly repeat the words "I Am," to assist you, while thinking about what these words actually mean as you say them.

Your discomfort is a distortion of the consciousness of comfort, it is not separate from it. Since it's the same substance, one thing can be substituted for another at will via direct transformation.

You don't need to try and work out what is causing you to be unwell; retracing your emotional steps will only prolong your suffering. Simply start at the point of discomfort and transform it by viewing yourself through the eyes of love. Your condition—as already stated—is a distortion of truth; the truth is, you are healthy.

Ignore the aches and pains and continue to view your body through the filter of love. Appreciate yourself, enjoy yourself, and stop criticizing and judging your body, no matter its present physical condition. Steady your attention in order to give it intensity. The awareness you wish to join with at this point is health and freedom from pain and fear. Begin to feel "I Am healthy."

Stop desiring health by taking your attention away from anything that denies it, and allow it to take over your consciousness. At the height of intensity you are in agreement with being well, and in a short time, in some cases instantaneously, you will demonstrate the state of health you want.

If you are not facing a serious illness but want more energy, or you are concerned about your weight, follow the same guidance. You cannot view your body through the eyes of judgment, for judgment is in league with fear and can only distort your expressions.

❂

If you are presently under the care of a health professional, that is quite all right. Any treatment you are receiving has nothing to do with this. There is no need to give up your medications. They have their role to play.

The two methods of addressing your health issues are not made to complement one another, because the awareness of one is the sleep of the other. Remember, to see objectively you must be blind subjectively, and vice versa.

Metaphysical work, having not a thing to do with the world of medical science, does not impinge upon your relationship with your doctor. By all means go to your appointments, take your medication, follow your diet plan, but allow a quiet reverential calmness born of confidence to take root and build in you. Know that the doctor in charge of your care is not your God (human imagination), and that, whatever the prognosis may be, there is no medical condition that cannot be completely cured.

Depending upon your level of experience and self-confidence, you may wish to prove to yourself that there is nothing that cannot be achieved with a shift in consciousness. But be mindful of those around you who love you and may be concerned. Do not worry them by stubbornly refusing to follow their advice. If they wish you to seek medical care, satisfy them; it does nothing to stop the wonder-working power within you.

Don't argue, go within, hear them exclaiming at the miraculous change that has taken place in you.

It is all about agreement with the state of consciousness of health. If you fail to attain it, there will be nothing that even the brightest medical minds can do; but if you succeed, no prognosis or sentence of death can stop the transformative power of God (human imagination) from making you whole.

CHAPTER 21

If in Doubt,
Do the Loving Thing

You may be unaware that your creative use of imagination can be used to assist others. You can bring about changes in the personal circumstance of someone you know, cure sickness, or elevate them out of a state of despondency, all by applying the principles detailed throughout this book.

Whenever you think of a person other than yourself with feeling, you are setting in motion a sequence of events that must be followed to completion, which is the point of physical reality. Remember, all thoughts that are felt are capable of producing effects, and this applies to negative thoughts as well as positive. The effects are sometimes seen in an alarmingly short time because the one you are thinking about is in a hypnotic state relative to you, thereby giving no resistance to the manifestation process.

To use your imagination unlovingly is to set yourself up for torment because you are operating the faculties of your mind under the influence of fear.

Anger, hatred, resentment, all of these are the by-products of an unloving imagination and will in due course bring about destructive and potentially ruinous outcomes in the lives of all concerned. Do not be deceived; if you are capable of wishing harm on others, harm will most certainly come to you. In fact, whatever you wish of others will have its effect on you, because we give what we are conscious of being, and only that.

If you form the habit of thinking only good of others, only good can be thought of you, and you are free of the subjective influence exerted by external negative thinking.

Exercise

Bring to mind a friend, a relative, or some other whom you know to be in need of a particular thing. You may contact them via subjective control or otherwise mentally meet them at some familiar location. Fully immerse into the scene.

Hear your friend or the person you have met telling you of their good fortune, remark on how well they look, or congratulate them on some new success. Make the conversation as real as possible.

As you are listening, breathe in the familiar deep, rhythmic, generative way. You should continue the conversation up to the point of eruption. Take your attention away from your imaginal activity, knowing that the work has been done, and wait to hear about the good that you have set in motion.

The Bible explains that God's word cannot return to him void. What this means in Metaphysical terms is that your imaginal acts will always bear fruit, either for you or someone else.

On occasion, when exercising your imagination lovingly on behalf of another, the individual may be resistive to change or feel themselves unready to let go of their body of beliefs. Do not worry; because of the principle that God's word cannot return to him void, whatever you have sent out will return back to you in greater measure.

Don't give up. Persist in doing good for others, because you are doing good for yourself.

Similarly, if you send out some evil thought or desire, the effects are just as capable of returning back to you.

None of us really think that we're unkind or vindictive, but until we are able to uncritically observe our reactions to life we will fail to notice those aspects of our nature that are just that. The process of uncritical observation also lends a hand in the reshaping of our awareness, enabling us to change the undesirable attributes that lead to our difficulties and struggles.

"Do unto others as you would have them do unto you" helps in maintaining a healthy new attitude.

There is no imaginative deed that does not have an effect on some level, so to ensure that you reap only good, sow only good, for what you sow, you will inevitably reap.

As you progress in your work, don't allow your former habits to creep back in. Completely discard the old ways of thinking and speaking, as they will only lead to setbacks. Tell yourself that negative thinking and wishing ill of others belongs to the old you. The new you is a person of resplendence who is only capable of being kind.

A person incapable of listening to horrible corrupt things cultivates for themselves a life of loveliness even in the midst of turmoil and distress. You will find the tremors of the world don't touch you. You are unshaken in times of uncertainty and continue to make progress in everything you do.

You Are I Am

WHEN ALL IS said and done, we will all discover ourselves to be Christ, for there is only one spirit. This means that, regardless of physical background or religious belief, you and I, and every other man, woman, and child who exists, will conclude our journey with this discovery.

In this state of divine unity no one outranks the other; there is only one Lord and Father of all and you will know yourself to be he who is God himself!

Do not be afraid to claim your position as God himself. Christ counted it not robbery to be equal with God, and neither should you. Your human imagination is the substance from which everything is made. It doesn't matter how many billions of things exist in the world, or how many thrilling new discoveries are made every day. There are infinite discoveries yet to be made because consciousness is infinite.

Limiting God to some little icon is beneath you once you discover the truth of who you really are for yourself.

No matter how many portraits of Christ get painted, they will never represent Christ, for Christ was never a man who existed; he is the final psychological state we occupy before incorporation. Christ is our awareness of being.

The Bible is not a religious text. That is why there are so many interpretations of it making the world none the wiser as to the meaning of its content. The Bible is your autobiography. It holds knowledge about every psychological state available to man, albeit layered in a way that does require spiritual revelation in order for its meaning to be made clear to you. It is a practical document that can be handled by anyone and will be revealed to everyone. You don't need to be particularly good, or lovely; you just need to feel after its true meaning and wait for an answer.

But do not be concerned with that. Put first things first. If you are hungry for a spiritual awakening, prove the Father by calling into physical existence the products of your imaginative mind, stir up the gift in you. Put your imagination to the test and the promise of God to you will be fulfilled in its own good time.

ABOUT THE AUTHOR

© Kassie Dowling

KATE JEGEDE is a British television host and author with a background in science. She was first introduced to Metaphysics as a teenager by her mother, a former yoga teacher and education specialist. She developed a penetrating and enduring fondness for the self-empowering teachings of Neville Goddard, and remains steadfastly devoted to spreading his message to this day. After completing her studies, Kate moved to Switzerland to work at the World Health Organization, developing educational resources for rural communities in sub-Saharan Africa. In addition to her academic science career, Kate has worked with the BBC Science Unit and BBC Radio Oxford, and served as news editor of the international journal *Africa Health*, for which she conducted research trips, helping set up a learning resources and study center at one of Nigeria's forefront teaching hospitals. She has been published in the internationally acclaimed science journal *Nature*. Kate has also hosted two science series aimed at young adults for Channel 4 in the UK, earning a BAFTA nomination. She is married and lives in London.